Introducing Continents

Anita Ganeri

raintree

a Capstone company — publishers for children

Raintree is an imprint of Capstone Global Library Limited, a company incorporated in England and Wales having its registered office at 7 Pilgrim Street, London, EC4V 6LB – Registered company number: 6695582

www.raintreepublishers.co.uk
myorders@raintreepublishers.co.uk

Text © Capstone Global Library Limited 2014
First published in hardback in 2014
Paperback edition first published in 2015
The moral rights of the proprietor have been asserted.

Edited by Dan Nunn, Rebecca Rissman, Sian Smith, and Helen Cox Cannons
Designed by Philippa Jenkins
Original illustrations © Capstone Global Library Ltd 2014
Picture research by Liz Alexander and Tristan Leverett
Production by Vicki Fitzgerald
Originated by Capstone Global Library Ltd
Printed and bound in China by Leo Paper Products Ltd

ISBN 978 1 406 26293 3 (hardback)
17 16 15 14 13
10 9 8 7 6 5 4 3 2 1

ISBN 978 1 406 26302 2 (paperback)
18 17 16 15
10 9 8 7 6 5 4 3

British Library Cataloguing in Publication Data
Ganeri, Anita
Introducing Asia. – (Introducing continents)
A full catalogue record for this book is available from the British Library.

Acknowledgements
We would like to thank the following for permission to reproduce photographs: Alamy p. 16 (© Shivang Mehta); Getty Images pp. 13 (Noel Celis/AFP), 17 (Mint Images/ Frans Lanting), 18 (Marketa Jirouskova/ Oxford Scientific); Shutterstock pp. 6 (© Alexandra Lande), 7 (© Anastasios71), 8 (© my-summit), 9 (© David Steele), 10 (© stephen Rudolph), 11 (© ekipaj), 12 (© alersandr hunta), 14 (© Sergey Uryadnikov), 15 (© silver-john), 19 (© LIN, CHUN-TSO), 20 (© Dmitry Berkut), 21 (© shupian), 22 (© Hinochika), 23 (© Dana Ward), 25 (© Svilen G), 26 (© Stasis Photo), 27 (© Thomas La Mela).

Cover photographs of mountains in China, a Chinese New Year lion dance, and a shaded relief map all reproduced with permission of Shutterstock (© Vixit, © windmoon, © AridOcean).

Contents

Some words are shown in bold, **like this**. You can find out what they mean by looking in the glossary.

About Asia

A **continent** is a huge area of land. There are seven continents on Earth. This book is about the continent of Asia. Asia is the biggest continent.

ARCTIC OCEAN

North America

Europe

MEDITERRANEAN SEA

Asia

ATLANTIC OCEAN

Africa

PACIFIC OCEAN

Equator

PACIFIC OCEAN

South America

INDIAN OCEAN

Australia

SOUTHERN OCEAN

Antarctica

Asia stretches from the Mediterranean Sea in the west to the Pacific Ocean in the east. To the north is the Arctic Ocean. In the west, Asia is linked to the continent of Europe.

Asia fact file	
Area	about 43,820,000 square kilometres (16,918,996 square miles)
Population	over 4,000 million
Number of countries	50
Highest mountain	Mount Everest at 8,850 metres (29,035 feet)
Longest river	Yangtze at 6,300 kilometres (3,915 miles)

Famous places

Asia has many famous places. Some are very old. The Taj Mahal in India was built more than 400 years ago. The **emperor** of India built it as a **tomb** for his wife.

The beautiful Taj Mahal is built from white marble.

Inside the Burj Khalifa are flats and offices.

Some famous places are very modern. The Burj Khalifa in Dubai, in the United Arab Emirates, was opened in 2010. It is almost 830 metres (2,723 feet) high – the tallest building in the world.

Geography

Asia has many different **landforms**. The Himalayas are found to the north of India and Nepal. They are the highest mountains on Earth. Mount Everest is the world's highest mountain. It stands 8,850 metres (29,035 feet) tall.

Many climbers visit the Himalayas every year.

Ural Mountains

Pamirs

Karakoram Range

Kunlun Mountains

Mount Everest

Himalayas

| 0 | 1275 | miles |
| 0 | 2050 | km |

8

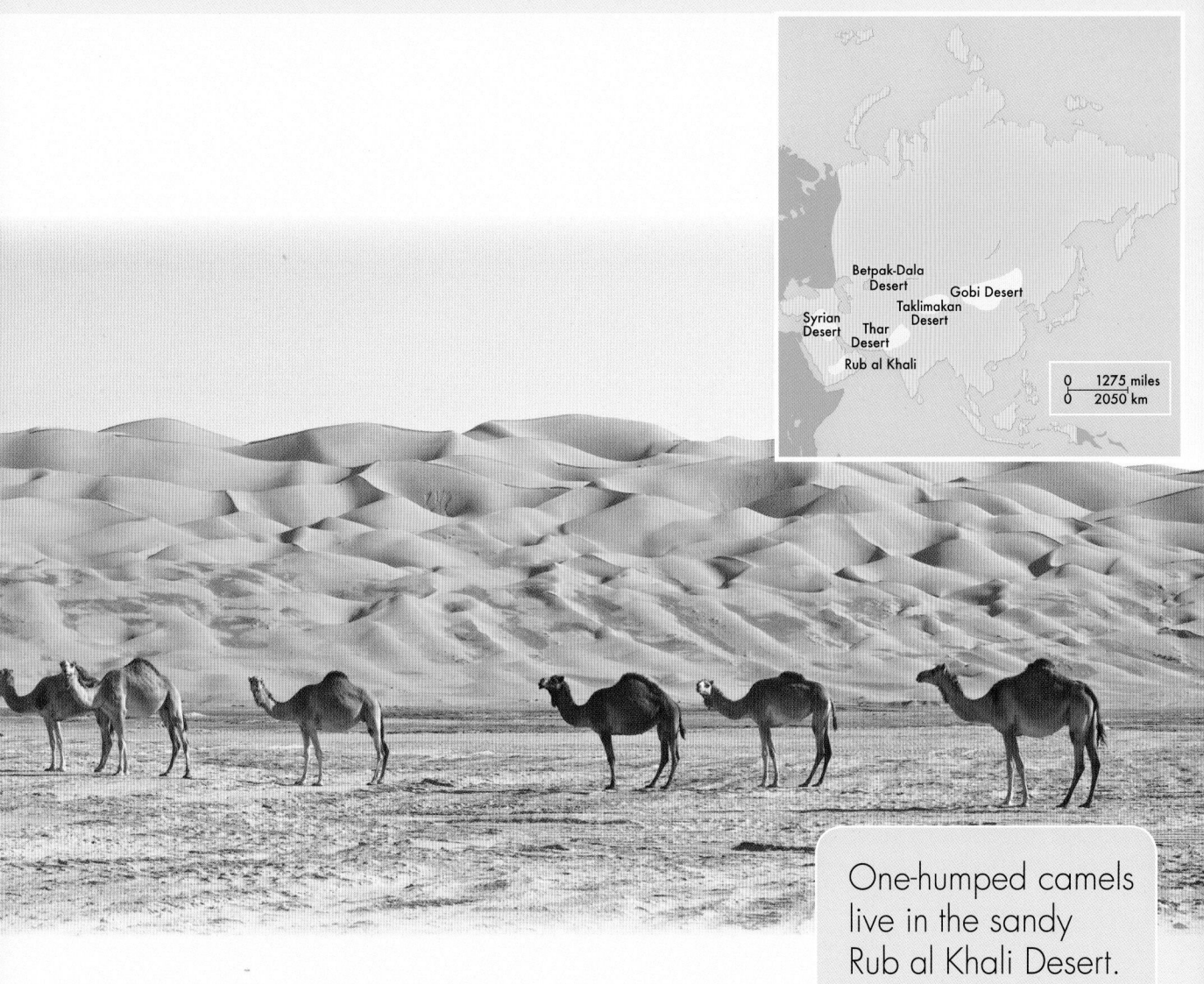

One-humped camels
live in the sandy
Rub al Khali Desert.

There are enormous deserts in Asia.
The rocky Gobi Desert lies in China and
Mongolia. It is very hot in summer and
very cold in winter. The sandy Rub al Khali
Desert is in the Arabian Peninsula.

9

The Yangtze River in China is the longest river in Asia. It flows for 6,300 kilometres (3,915 miles) from the mountains in western China to the East China Sea. Millions of people live along the riverbanks.

The Yangtze River is very important for water, food, and transport.

Over 130 rivers flow into the Caspian Sea, including the River Volga.

Asia also has many large lakes. The Caspian Sea, between Asia and Europe, is the biggest lake on Earth. It covers 371,000 square kilometres (143,000 square miles). It is called a sea because its water is salty.

Weather

Asia is so big that it has a wide range of weather. There are rainforests in South East Asia. They lie around the **equator**, where it is always hot and wet. In the far north of Russia, it is freezing cold all year round.

It is so cold in Siberia, Russia, that the ground is always frozen.

Arctic Circle

Key
Wet
Desert
Cold

0   1,275 miles
0   2,050 km

Equator

Typhoons cause terrible damage in the Philippines.

Each year, **monsoon** winds bring heavy rains to countries such as India. Some parts of Asia are hit by fierce storms, called **typhoons**. These can cause flooding that can wash away people's homes and crops.

Animals

Many amazing animals live in Asia. Orang-utans live in the rainforests on the islands of Borneo and Sumatra. Komodo dragons live in Indonesia. They are the world's biggest lizards and can grow up to 3 metres (10 feet) long.

Komodo dragons only live on a few islands in Indonesia.

Giant pandas are easy to spot with their striking black-and-white coats.

Giant pandas live in south central China. They mostly eat **bamboo**. Giant pandas are very rare. Today, there are only about 1,500 left in the wild because their forest homes are being cut down.

Plants

Mangrove **swamps** grow along the coasts of India and Bangladesh, where rivers flow into the sea. The trees have long roots to help them keep a firm hold in the mud.

Large mangrove swamps grow around the Bay of Bengal.

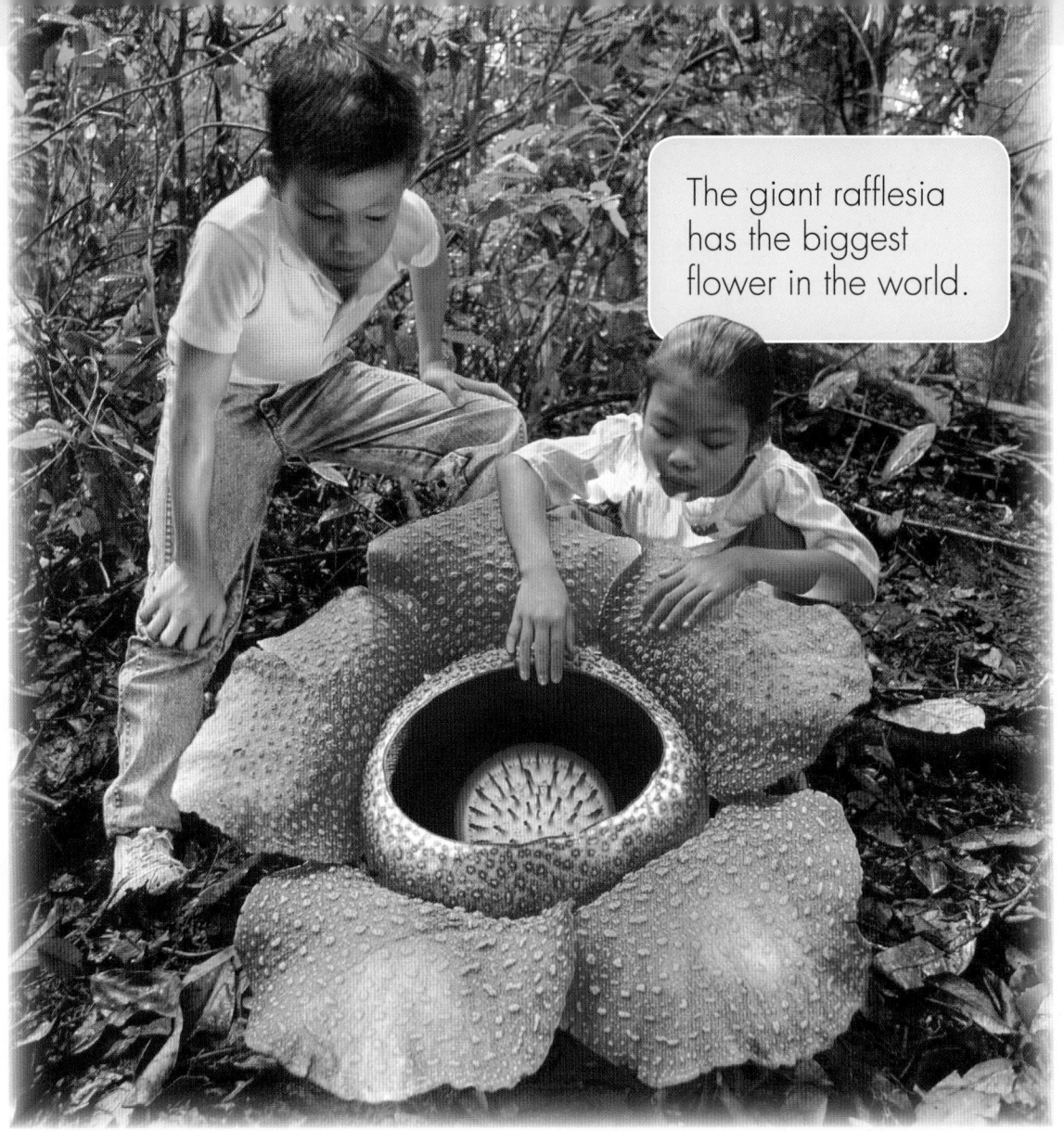

The giant rafflesia has the biggest flower in the world.

A huge forest of pine, fir, and larch trees stretches across the north of Asia. Warm, wet rainforests grow in South East Asia. The rafflesia is a rainforest plant. Its giant flower smells like rotting meat.

Natural resources

Asia has many **natural resources**. Much of the world's oil comes from the Middle East. The oil comes from under the desert. The countries in the Middle East sell their oil around the world. Selling oil has made them very rich.

These oil wells are in the desert in the Middle Eastern country of Qatar.

Many farmers in Asia still harvest their crops by hand.

There are many farms, both large and small, across Asia. Rice is grown in flooded fields, called **paddy fields**. Farmers also grow tea, rubber, wheat, cotton, and sugar cane.

People

Over 4,000 million people live in Asia. This is about three out of every five people on Earth. China and India are the most crowded countries. Very few people live in Mongolia.

People crowd along the banks of the River Ganges in India.

This is Chinese writing. The letters and sounds are called characters.

The people of Asia speak thousands of different languages. Many people speak more than one language. More than 1,000 million people speak Mandarin Chinese. Some local languages only have a few speakers.

Culture and sport

Many colourful festivals take place across Asia. Each spring, Japanese people celebrate when the cherry trees blossom. They visit parks to see the cherry trees, light lanterns, and have picnics under the trees.

These people in Japan are enjoying the beautiful cherry blossom.

Many people play cricket in India and Pakistan.

Many sports are played in Asia. Cricket is very popular in India, Pakistan, Bangladesh, and Sri Lanka. **Martial arts**, such as judo and kung fu, are common in Japan, China, and North and South Korea.

Countries

There are 50 countries in Asia. The smallest country is the Maldives. It is a group of tiny islands in the Indian Ocean. Indonesia is made up of more than 18,000 islands. It is the world's largest group of islands.

1. Russia
2. Georgia
3. Armenia
4. Azerbaijan
5. Turkey
6. Cyprus
7. Lebanon
8. Israel
9. Jordan
10. Syria
11. Iraq
12. Saudi Arabia
13. Yemen
14. Oman
15. United Arab Emirates
16. Kuwait
17. Iran
18. Turkmenistan
19. Uzbekistan
20. Kazakhstan
21. Kyrgyzstan
22. Tajikistan
23. Afghanistan
24. Pakistan
25. India
26. Sri Lanka
27. Nepal
28. Bangladesh
29. Bhutan
30. Myanmar
31. Thailand
32. Cambodia
33. Malaysia
34. Vietnam
35. Laos
36. Brunei
37. Indonesia
38. Singapore
39. China
40. Taiwan
41. Mongolia
42. North Korea
43. South Korea
44. Japan
45. Maldives
46. Bahrain
47. East Timor
48. Qatar
49. Philippines
50. Occupied Palestinian Territory

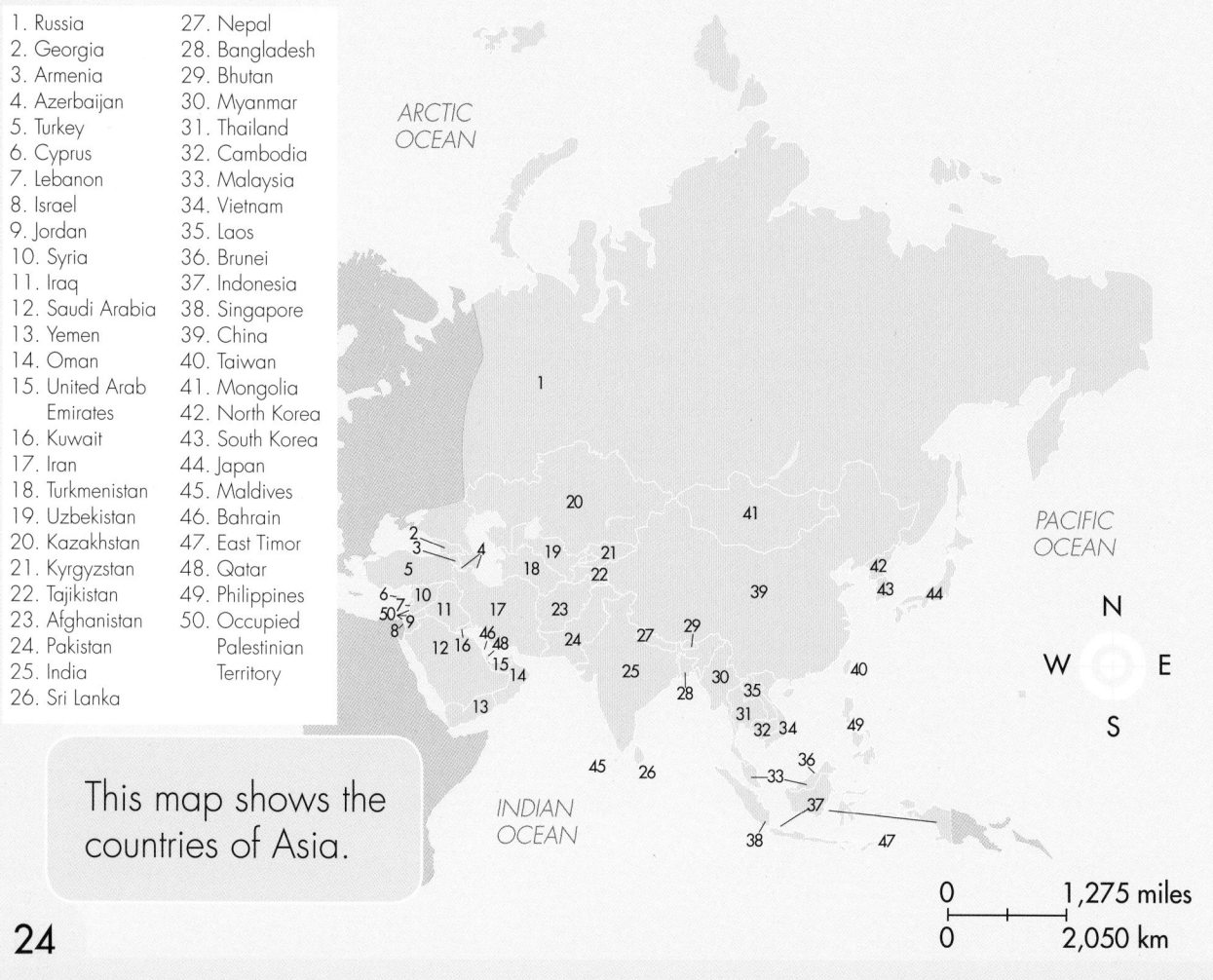

This map shows the countries of Asia.

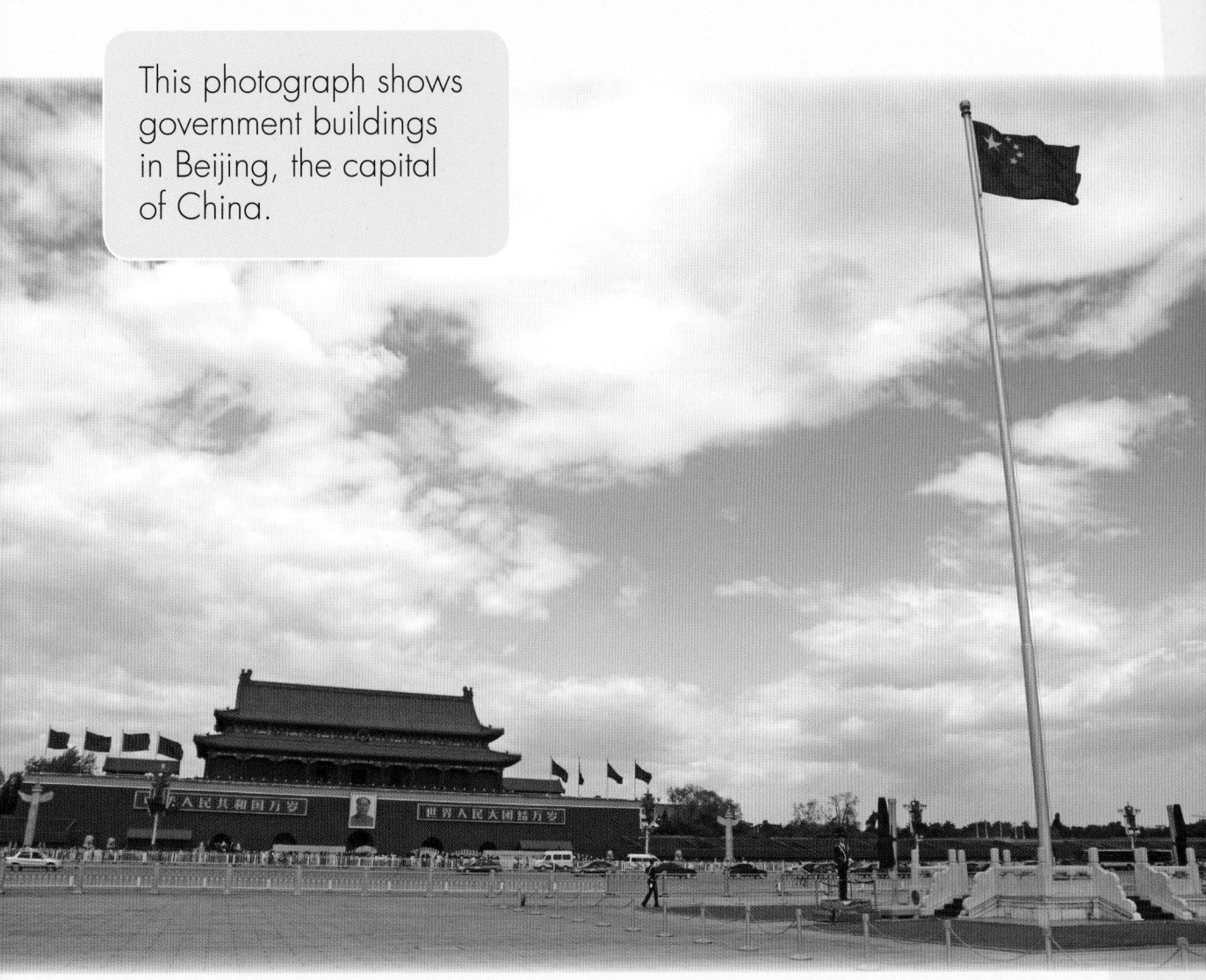

This photograph shows government buildings in Beijing, the capital of China.

China is the biggest country that is just in Asia. Russia is bigger but only part of Russia is in Asia. The other part is in the **continent** of Europe. Turkey is also split between Asia and Europe.

Countryside and cities

In the countryside in Asia, many people still live in small villages. Some villages do not have running water or electricity. Each year, many people move from the countryside to the cities to look for work.

This small village is in Thailand. Many people who live here get food and money from fishing.

This crowded street is in Tokyo, the capital of Japan.

Asia has some very big, crowded cities. Among the biggest are Shanghai in China, Mumbai in India, and Tokyo in Japan.

Fun facts

- Asia takes up almost one-third of all the land on Earth.

- Lake Baikal in Russia is the deepest lake on Earth. It plunges to more than 1,600 metres (5,249 feet).

- China and Russia have more neighbours than any other countries. China and Russia both have borders with 14 countries.

- The 10 highest mountains in the world are all found in Asia.

Quiz

1. Which building in Asia is the tallest in the world?

2. Which plant do giant pandas like to eat?

3. Which is the smallest country in Asia?

4. Which mountain in Asia is the highest in the world?

4. Mount Everest

3. The Maldives

2. Bamboo

1. The Burj Khalifa in Dubai

Glossary

bamboo tall plant with thin, woody stems

continent one of seven huge areas of land on Earth

emperor person who rules an empire

equator imaginary line running around the middle of Earth

landforms features, such as mountains, on Earth's surface

martial arts sports such as judo and karate

monsoon wind that brings heavy rain

natural resources natural materials that we use, such as wood, coal, oil, and rock

paddy fields flooded fields where rice is grown

swamps places where the ground is muddy or flooded

tomb place where a dead body is put

typhoons fierce storms that bring strong winds and heavy rain

Find out more

Books

Asia (Continents of the World), Rob Bowden (Wayland, 2007)

Asia (Exploring Continents), Anita Ganeri (Heinemann Library, 2008)

Horrible Geography of the World, Anita Ganeri (Scholastic, 2010)

Websites to visit

kids.discovery.com/tell-me/people-and-places/our-7-continents
Various games, puzzles, and activities about the seven continents can be found on this website.

kids.nationalgeographic.com/kids/games/geographygames/copycat
This fun game helps you to find the continents on a map of the world.

www.worldatlas.com
This site has lots of maps, facts, and figures about Asia.

Index